Table of Contents

Chapter One...   Warning   Page 2

Chapter Two...   Hope to Promise: Mental Conditioning   Page 4

Chapter Three...   The Program: Day 1-30.   Page 10

Chapter One: Warning

Natural Health Program-10 Minute Workout for Optimal Health

WARNING: You must be completely willing to attain the best health for your life, and to do this you must not only believe it is possible, but that it is essential to your beliefs AND values. The need for Natural Health must be integral to your being. You must be able to focus on what is most important to you. You must have faith that 10 minutes of exercise for 30 days will help you gain Natural Health.

Essential: Increase water consumption, or fruit and vegetable consumption, for proper hydration when increasing activity levels within this program. Sleep, rest, meditate or pray to rejuvenate the body and recover from workouts.

You must turn hope into promise. You have hope if you are reading this, and when you complete this program for 30 days, your hope will turn into promise. Let me be clear, it is not the program... It is your miraculous body and mind that is capable of much more than we can ever imagine. This program is designed to include as many muscles as possible, and use the most effective methods of training that is studied in university and used by top trainers and athletes.

All you have to do is focus your will power for ten minutes to utilize your other super power... the power of accomplishment. This may even take more than one try, and you may need to make other improvements in your life such as sleep, emotional healing through forgiveness of others and yourself, hydration with more pure water (distilled), more fruits and vegetables in their raw state, and/or less refined food (including salt and oil). You can do anything you are willing to put your mind to and work for.

Only 10% of people who read books make it past the first chapter. Be that 10%. This program is very short and simple. It is meant to only take ten minutes per day for thirty days, which sounds easy yet is a large feat that will bring you dramatically phenomenal results. Our bodies are miraculous. Let that miracle shine with ten minutes of work per day.

You are not paying for the hours it took me to write this, nor the minutes it takes to create and perform the best workouts in the world… you are investing in the decades of research through education, experience, and passion it took me to get to this point.

This Natural Health Program is a revolutionary technology that is challenging for me to release as a book because of its immense power to transcend one's current fitness level. It is a simple task due to the innate power of a human being, yet the simplicity is often taken for granted as one of the many miracles of life. If you purchased this program, it is certainly worth hundreds of dollars, if not thousands, so it is a challenge for me to sell this at a rate which a "book" is sold for. My mission here on Earth is to teach excellence, and fitness is an essential part of that, and this my dear reader… is priceless.

CHAPTER TWO... HOPE TO PROMISE

I am going to spare as much excessive writing as possible to make this program as pure and essential as it can be. We will begin a 30 day journey in which you will feel your Natural Health increase every day. If you are reading word by word with sincerity, then you must already feel a rush of Natural Health. You are capable of producing your own internal chemicals that are the same chemicals used in the most potent muscle relaxants and painkillers available.

If you do not think 30 days is enough, consider that if any athlete took 30 days off, they would greatly deteriorate their performance and fitness gains. This is called reversibility. If you think 10 minutes is too little of a duration, calculate the actual time spent exercising when people go to a gym for one hour practicing eight (30 second) exercises with three sets to total about 12 minutes of actual exercise. If people socialize and practice isolating exercises, or do not stress the muscle enough to properly contract the muscle, more time is spent inefficiently.

What you will need for this Natural Health Program:
- Enough will to do consistent work.
- Enough sleep, rest, and nutrition (most importantly enough water and fruit).
- 10 minutes for 30 consecutive days (no breaks).
- A timer or stopwatch and no other equipment.

Practicing compound movement exercises in an anaerobic state with a focus on specificity causes adaptation. It is the most effective and efficient way of training. This program is not aimed to be technical, it is intended to have the least words possible with proper instruction. These words in bold explain much of what (the secret trick) is outlined in textbooks, and this program is that wisdom in practice.

I do not wish to include anything about nutrition, as it is a comprehensive subject that needs its own "program". One thing I must include to make this Natural Health Program successful is the addition of fruit in the diet. Vegetables are also essential (it is best to increase vegetable intake also) yet fruit contains the perfectly needed amount of carbohydrates for exercise and vitamin C (fruit is the best source of vitamin C possible). Exercise is much more difficult without a proper amount of carbohydrates in the diet (carbs fuel all cells). Just as exercise is challenging without water, and it is borderline dangerous not to advise drinking more water if exercising. Water and carbohydrates are two of our six essential nutrients. It would also be dangerous to allow only 5 hours of sleep for a growing child, we are not nocturnal animals and need to sleep at night (9-12 hours) for proper development, and this holds true for adults - especially when active.

Vitamin C (along with other essential nutrients) is absolutely needed for recovery and optimal performance. It is so important I would go as far as to inform you about vitamin C crystals (best with fresh orange juice) to ensure intake if your fruit consumption is low (less than 5 fist-sized servings per day), although nothing can replace or compare to the loads of nutrients within a single piece of fruit.

Books and studies are filled with reasons to exercise. Research the phrase "100 reasons to exercise" and you will refresh and deepen your inspiration and will to train hard.

Here is a list of just a few well documented benefits for exercise relevant to this program:
- ☐ Decrease all risks of disease for men and women
- ☐ Improve bladder and bowel control (avoid urine, gas and stool leakage) in just weeks
- ☐ Increase overall self-confidence and quality of life

- Reduce the risk of death in women and men
- In women, improve recovery from childbirth and gynecological surgery
- In men, improve long-term prostate health and recovery after prostate surgery
- Spend less muscular energy during sex and increase overall endurance in intimate moments
- Intake more oxygen from the air
- Reduce and/or prevent back pain
- Reduce and/or prevent sarcopenia which is the loss of 1% of muscle mass, and a decrease in bone density, tendon, and ligament around the age of 30.

Based on the results my students achieved with this method, I can confidently say that you will achieve maximum depth squat and push up in approximately 11 to 28 days. Plus, if you follow this program to the point, you will be able to display full strength and endurance anytime without a warm up, even if:

-You're not an athlete or not in great physical condition
-You're over 40, 50, 60 or 70-years young
-You haven't practiced any sport before
-You are man or woman
-You don't have any previous training or experience
-You did a lot of heavy lifting, cycling or running in the past
-You think that your hips or knees are too weak, and in pain or inflamed
-You think you are too old to achieve great strength or endurance

In reality you are already over 50% on your way if you can get up from a chair. The missing link is progressive repetition of exercises and doing sets with the most effective exercises, NOT duration of time or experience. We all have human bodies capable of amazing feats regardless of age, weight, or athletic ability.

Let's face it, your body is designed for intense exercise and loads of activity, not to sit for hours daily. Your body is designed to move, and although it will feel very uncomfortable and it is a great challenge to persist for 30 days, it will be more valuable than anything in your life. Increasing health IS life as it increases the ability to enjoy life.

This program is a prescription with specific repetitions, or time intervals, for specific exercises with alternatives available. It is designed to meet everyone's needs as we are all more alike than different. Hospitals treat people very similar, and this is also done with exercise prescription. It does not take very long to get into great shape, we are designed for activity. A squat and a push up are not the most difficult exercises, nor is a split, it is only that we do not practice these exercises regularly.

It is very important that you do not push past any pain. There are two aspects that are more than enough to look for: breathing heavy and feeling the burn. Fitness gains are not about feeling any pain. Pain is a sign to stop what you are doing and tend to the pain. You can always start the program at a later time after recovery. As long as you stop if you feel pain, and you are always able to breathe enough to speak a full sentence, you will not rip, tear, or injure yourself. Focus on proper form and be sure to apply a warm up and cool down as advised, and longer if needed.

It is also very important to create a distinction between the two phases (or part one and two) of an exercise (concentric and eccentric, as will be explained briefly later in the book). This prevents any "bouncing" during a strength training exercise to avoid risk for injury, as one unknowingly is loading much more weight, and may also break form.

Our first practice will be breath control. Finding a comfortable place, such as touching the Earth in Nature, or lying down and in a quiet, dark room, is very helpful but not essential as this can be practiced anywhere. Breathe in deep for 5-10 seconds, hold for 5-10 seconds, and then breathe out for 5-10 seconds. The exact time is very important, yet it is much more important that you start your practice at whatever level (between 5-10 seconds) you are currently at. Practice at least once a day, and schedule this time at a point in the day that you can spare, so much that you do not forget to do this daily. Doing this 3-5 times a day can dramatically increase benefits, especially during times of stress, yet it is again much more important that you begin and are consistent. So, for now, focus on once per day.

One quick story before we move on to your second practice of breath control. When I ask people to guess how many push ups the world record holder did to get the title, no one comes close to guessing 7,000. This was done by a high school kid who did 123 push ups when tested one day and he was upset because he knew he had done much more previously. He decided to create a standard. He did 123 push ups daily until he felt up to it, and then held the next standard of 222, then 444 push ups per day until he reached this unthinkable goal of 7,000 which he said he could even do more yet the person testing him became concerned for his safety! The point of this story is not to replicate this training technique. In fact, most exercise science is contrary to his unique results. The point of this story is not only to hold a standard for yourself, it is that we are capable of what we are willing to work for and enjoy the journey due to the importance we hold for the value of our belief.

Another amazing story is the life of [Wim Hoff](). He is a great example of Natural Health and has an extremely effective breathing technique. It is also very simple to practice, at least one part of it. Again, being comfortable is important, and also being in a safe place as lightheadedness is known to occur for many people due to increased oxygen intake and blood flow (along with the chemicals mentioned that are produced internally). Breath in as deeply as possible, then let go of the breath with no force, then again after you exhale breath in with force as deeply as possible, repeat this for 30 breaths and then breathe in as deeply as possible for a long breath hold (1-2 minutes if possible or as long as you can comfortably). You can do this one to three times.

These two examples of breath control are very powerful. There are many more, but these two hold enormous power and there are even studies proving it. Some of the most powerful evidence is within footage of Wim Hoff, yet there is also plenty of research with studies showing huge benefits for Natural Health such as balancing blood pressure, diabetes, heart disease, and other traumatic diseases. Practice at least one of these techniques daily and increase as much as you are willing to increase your health.

Do not forget to place that seed of Natural Health when breathing deeply, and do it throughout the day as much as possible. One simple way to create this consistent focus on healing and health is simply repeating these words: "Health and healing! Love and gratitude, strength and Healing, purity and cleanliness. " These words are very powerful and a quick way to redirect focus when one loses track and fumbles with negative thoughts. Create your own two words that stimulate your feelings of wellness and goodness. If you wish to further your willingness to repeat words (inaudible or quietly is just as effective), watch footage on, or read books by Dr. Emoto. Dr. Emoto studied the impact of positive words, especially Love and Gratitude, by freezing water in a petri dish and documenting the water crystals shape becoming symmetric (this is how we recognize beauty) and negative words like hate become asymmetrical.

Now we will begin our first day of training. This will be a simple ten minutes every day, with no equipment needed.

Every day of this Program You will increase:
- Cardiovascular Endurance
- Muscular Strength and Endurance
- Flexibility

CHAPTER THREE... THE PROGRAM: DAY 1-30

DAY 1: Testing and setting a standard

*Day one has much more reading than any other day. It is okay to read this book one day at a time, or the entire book more than once. Whichever way you choose will be extremely effective as long as you practice daily for 30 days. You can consider 30 consecutive days of exercise similar to that of watering a newly planted tree; it takes some time for the roots to grow and the tree to adapt and then it does not need daily watering.

All workouts may benefit you more if you practice outside with bare feet (footwear prevents this due to a rubber sole) in contact with the Earth. This has been studied with peer review journals to have a positive effect on one's health and is called "grounding". We do conduct electrical currents in our bodies and there is no negative side effect to being in contact with the Earth. It is also very helpful to have fresh air during workouts as indoor areas harbor many pollutants such as synthetic chemicals, formaldehyde, carbon monoxide, and environmental tobacco smoke even in the cleanest of homes.

Sit in a chair with your arms extended forward. Notice how the hips draw back and the knees do not go forward. Stand up from the chair making sure to fully extend the joints of the knees and hips. Repeat this as many times as you can with as good of form as your first few repetitions. Write this number down or document it electronically now with the date. It is best to have an entire notebook dedicated to your Natural Health Journey.

If you can do over 50 repetitions, you may remove the chair and squat like a toddler, which is the best description of a squat possible, being sure to let the calf touch the hamstring on every repetition. This is the preferred squat and what is possible for almost everyone, but there is no reason to rush the process. It is much more important to create a standard for yourself and consistently progress with daily practice.

If you cannot sit in a chair without pain, simply adjust the range of motion to only one inch, pushing your hips back. As you push your hips back, lift your arms above your head and, as you stand up, fully extend your legs (hips and knees) "throwing" an imaginary basketball to the ground. This imaginary basketball can also be thought of as a stress ball with all of your worries and tension in it, and as you throw it down to the ground you remove it from your body. In the end phase of this squat, your hands are behind your body, fully extended, with fingers pointed towards the ground. You can progress by reaching a higher number of repetitions, such as 50 or 100 at a certain range of motion such as one inch, then progress to a two inch squat, then three, until you reach the destination of a full squat.

Take note of how long this exercise took and how much exertion it caused. The heavy breathing is a sign of oxygen debt, which means that you are burning glucose which greatly helps balance blood sugars levels protecting oneself from diabetes (which affects an estimated 25% of the population and is predicted to be the future for 1 out of 3 of the children, 1 out of 2 of ethnic descent, born after the year 2000 - Centers for Disease Control). If you are not breathing heavy and feel no burning sensation localized to your legs (which is lactic acid), you may not have pushed yourself to your sub maximal effort. It is very important to push yourself to "sub maximal effort" which basically means two things:

- ☐ BREATH HEAVY
- ☐ FEEL THE BURN

You may also experience localized shaking in the muscle during exercise, also during stretching if pushing to your maximum potential. This is okay as it is a sign of exertion. You should not feel lethargic or tired the following day as that is a sign of overtraining or malnutrition. Shaking in the entire body is also a sign of malnutrition: usually carbohydrates and/or potassium. Fruit is an excellent source of carbohydrates and potassium.

This exercise is very important. It is the foundation for humanity. Don't believe me? Simply look at a child do a squat thousands and thousands of times and you will see that I am not exaggerating. The toddler does this exercise perfectly and they are the greatest teacher of how to practice, so watch them on video if you cannot in person. You will get to this point, again, within days, if you can sit in a chair and are willing and faithful.

The up portion of the squat (getting back up) is certainly harder than getting down, but there is a secret to it! The down motion is the eccentric stage, and the up motion is the concentric stage. In the first phase of the squat, the eccentric stage, go slower with a one-two count on the way down, and on the way up, the concentric stage, go up faster with more power on a one count. Again, go down with a one-two count, and up with a one count.

Breathe as deeply as possible during exercise. Breath so deep that someone across the room can hear you audibly breathing. It may help to breathe out on the way up, but it is not needed and may interfere with a continuous cadence of repetitions. Doing the squat non stop is essential, with not even a one second break at the top when your legs are straight is permitted. You must squat continuously until you reach that point of breathing heavy and feeling the burn (anaerobic training) to reach maximum results.

Not reaching maximum results may result in reaching no results, because IF the gain is not massive for "working out" you probably won't work out!

You can count your average for one minute, once you progress to over 50 reps in one set (no break). Do not be hesitant to reach higher numbers in reps. If you average 25 reps per minute, 100 squats will only take 4 minutes. 4 minutes is often how long people rest for at a gym (even with a trainer). One thousand squats can be done in under 30 minutes. Many people spend 30 minutes driving one way to the gym. 1,000 squats may seem like an extremely high number. Within 30 days one can go from 10 squats to 100, or from 100 to 1,000 squats if practiced daily and consecutively. Do not be overwhelmed with numbers for optimal progression and performance. Focus on the 2 signs of exertion:

- Breathing Heavy and
- Feeling the Localized Burn in the Muscle

Your needs and conditioning change daily. Please be sensitive to your body and when you "feel good," perform more intense exercises such as increasing range of motion or increase repetitions and sets. On "off days" when you are not feeling as good, do LESS REPS and you will have higher net profits, meaning you will increase muscle strength more overall.

One more exercise for the day! It is just as simple and effective. It is also a foundation of humanity! Toddlers will do this exercise perfectly yet it is not extremely noticeable because it is constantly altered. If a toddler constantly witnesses a traditional push up, they will mimic it! Although the traditional push up is wonderful and will produce amazing results, it is not needed to practice this variety of a push ups to reap tremendous results!

We will be practicing a Hindu push up, also called a "dand". It has many names and is used in the military, martial arts, and hatha yoga. It works every muscle from head to toe, yet we generally consider it to work the upper body. The squat also works many more muscles than the legs, as in studies it shows to contract the abdominal wall more than a crunch.

The Dand:

First get in a pose very popular with our greatest exercise science teacher, a toddler, the pyramid position. Your hips are to be the highest point with your hands and feet on the ground. If this itself is painful simply put your hands on a higher surface such as a very sturdy table, chair, staircase, or wall. I prefer staircase but whatever is available daily is best. Get into this position, also called the pike position in gymnastics, and progressively work to keep your back straight. Look between your thumbs to enable the entire spine to remain stacked (straight). Video recording yourself every now and then will greatly aid in your proprioception, or knowing where your body is in space, so that the perfection of your form increases.

This pike position is the first step, then transition to the second step by gently lowering the hips to the ground with control and looking up (step two). Keep your arms extended throughout this motion, from step one to step two. Your hips are close to the ground along with your legs, but do not let your body touch the ground throughout the entire exercise. Pull your shoulders back and your shoulder blades together, "opening your heart" in this step two position.

From here you will use your core muscles (the muscles surrounding your spine, including your abdominals) to lift you back up into step one and repeat the exercise. If your range of motion is not as full as explained here, it is okay, it is much more important that you create a standard for yourself and continuously progress daily.

If you have been training or if this exercise is not too hard, practice it again adding a bend in the arms and an extension of the arms (elbows). To do this you will simulate diving into the ground and letting your forehead hover over the ground between your hands, followed by your chin, chest, hips, and then you extend your arms. If you cannot bend your arms so deeply as to almost touch your forehead to the ground, simply lessen the range of motion so that you only bend your arms one inch (just like with the squat). Altering the range of motion can be done not only as an alteration for a beginner, it can also be used on day where you are "feeling off" emotionally or if you are lacking sleep or nutrition.

Now that you have practiced this exercise a few times, see how many you can perform in one set as your "max". This is how many repetitions you can perform one after another with no rest. The form of the last repetition should be as good as the first few and, if it is not, this can greatly increase your risk of injury. Push yourself to breath heavy and feel the burn, but not to a point where you are risking injury.

Document the time and date, and how many squats and dands you completed in your Natural Health Journey Journal. Include how you feel on a 1-100 scale before and after your workout, and the duration (how long) of your workout. If the duration was less than ten minutes, be sure to spend the next few minutes practicing breath control.

Example of the Natural Health Journey Journal: (1-100 scale)

Exercise-Reps-Sets-Time/Date-Rate of ease-Emotional State: one word before & - after

Squat - 100 - 1 - 4min/10.14.19 - 33   -   frustrated - 44   happy - 89
Dand - 25 - 4 - 5min/10.14.19 - 52   -   angry   - 29   elated - 89

For Printing or Designing your own
Natural Health Journey Journal: (1-100 scale)

Exercise-Reps-Sets-Time/Date-Rate of ease-Emotional State: one word before & - after

DAY 2: Perfect Practice Makes Perfect

If you feel as if your muscles are sore, this is good as it is a sign of micro-tears in the muscle that are needed for growth. Being so sore that it interrupts daily function is not good, it is the opposite of what our goal is. Doing one set and testing for your max should not have this effect. If you feel "too" sore you may be dehydrated, lacking other nutrients, and/or sleep which is very dangerous.

It is important to drink more water when active, and in general. Guidelines for water consumption are to consume half your bodyweight in ounces. For example, if you weigh 200 pounds, you need to drink 100 ounces. This is a general guideline as increasing raw fruits and vegetables, and decreasing salt intake, greatly increases hydration levels.

Perform half of the reps you completed for the squat and the dand on day one with the same range of motion, or increase your range of motion if you are "feeling good".

Do this four times for each exercise.
This totals 8 sets: 4 sets of squats and 4 sets of dands.

This should take no longer than 8 minutes if there is no brake. The goal is to not take a break and go from one exercise, squat, to another, the dand. You most likely will take a few seconds to catch your breath, yet remember your values and beliefs and look at the timer. Realize you can do this for ten minutes.

DAY 3: Active recovery and cool down: Core and Stretching

Today you will perform two exercises and two stretches. First is the back extension. Lay on the floor with your chest to the ground and lift the chest with the lower back muscles, while keeping the legs and hips firmly planted on the ground. Put the ball of the foot on the ground, opposed to the shoelace, to further stabilize yourself. Your hands should be above your shoulders in a field goal position (U shape) and not touch the ground. If this is very challenging and painful, simply put your fingertips on the ground and assist a smaller range of motion. Your range of motion will increase daily with practice in this program. The most important thing is that you practice and create a standard for a range of motion. If you only move a millimeter, your muscles will contract in the same way as a trained athlete with a larger 5 inch range of motion if you are pushing yourself to your submaximal level of conditioning.

Practice this exercise until only 70-80% of your "max". Do not practice this exercise (the back extension) to your max until you are very accustomed to it as it is not worth risking being sore in the lumbar spine. This is a very powerful exercise as one of the few selected exercises in this program to make it simple and effective. Record how many repetitions you can do comfortably in your notebook.

Congratulations, you are creating new neurological pathways. This is called neurogenesis. Practicing these exercises, even with a smaller range of motion than you were hoping, IS creating new pathways for blood transport and nerve function. You are completing your goal.

From here you can practice your first stretch. The modified cobra. You will be in the same position, lay down on the ground with your chest to the ground. Lift your chest the same way, but use your arms and place (stack) your elbows directly under your shoulders. Look up from here to fully extend your spine. You can add to this stretch by pulling your shoulders back and your shoulder blades together, "opening your heart". This stretch should be relaxing and you can hold it for as long as 4 minutes, with a minimum of 30 seconds daily for optimal results, especially if you sit for hours a day. You can even read a book in this position and create net time, where two things are done at once.

You can make this stretch more challenging by extending your arms into full cobra, yet it is not needed and if done only 60 seconds is needed at most. This simple stretch can do wonders for the back IF done properly including the 4 minute prescription time.

The second exercise for today is an N up. This is a gymnastic exercise that we can easily modify as it is very challenging for most people. Sit on the floor and hug your legs, tell yourself "I love you" and realize that is the most important thing in your life, for without it there is not much worth living for. From this step one (hug yourself) position, place your hands on the ground to support your balance. Then extend your legs fully if possible, or extend your legs as far as you can "comfortably", while simultaneously laying down with the upper body. This is position two, balance and support your weight with your hands, preferably your fingertips for as little support as necessary. Optimally you will be laying down in this position. Adjust your range of motion according to your capabilities.

Step two, into step one, (from laying down to the self hug) is the harder motion and needs to be done with more force and speed. Keep your shoulders and knees level throughout the exercise, both joints remain the same height from the ground as they rise and lower from the ground. Perform as many repetitions as you can with all the focus you can muster. Record how many repetitions, the date, and how you feel from a 1-100 scale in your notebook. Realize that you are practicing a Russian methodology of training, called total body tension. This is using your body as a full unit as opposed to isolation exercises. This is a revolutionary method of training that you are practicing without being conscious of it due to the compound muscle exercises. Contracting so many muscles at once, and thinking about your body as a unit... a unit of elastic STEEL, because that is exactly what muscle is, it is so powerful it has never been synthesized.

Stretch number two is a split, since it looks so cool. It also greatly reduces pressure on the spine and nerves, which causes pain for many people. You will practice the split sitting on the ground. Place your feet directly in front of you and simply split them as far away from each other as you can with comfort.

One leg at a time place your hands as close to your foot as possible. Stretch as deep as you can, as close to your foot as possible for 10 seconds and then relax for 3 seconds. Contract the same muscle consciously with your mind for 5 seconds and then stretch again yet a bit further for 10 seconds. Again, contract your muscle consciously for 5 seconds and then stretch even a bit further for 10 seconds.

Be sure to use this exact time prescription for the stretch, as it is THE most effective stretching possible in studies in all my research and collegiate courses. Stretching is even documented as increasing injury and decreasing performance IF done before working out WITH long static holds (over 30 seconds to minutes long). So be sure to warm up before stretching, it is always used as a cool down, or rest period during intense exercise, within this program. The modified cobra can often be done with no warm up due to its low intensity. Do not practice the modified cobra with PNF (contacting) stretching.

For an increased challenge and deeper splits, practice this exercise standing in a split. As cool as a split is, not many want nor are willing to "do" a split. For this reason, doing this stretch on the ground is a great alternative, and one can turn the direction of the chest to face forward and stretch the obliques (side core muscles) more, or face the chest toward the ground and focus the stretch more on the lower back. The split can also be done one leg at a time if you are extremely inflexible and are not taking this program to increase your flexibility to the highest potential.

You can also practice side split and full splits for increased performance. For optimal flexibility, you may want to practice after every workout and include a PNF (tension) hip flexor stretch which is simply to hold a lunge with padding under your knee and place your knee on the padding. The total stretching time never needs to be over 5 minutes for a complete training protocol. You can also add a split exercise to be done on your back with legs in the air practicing a split in the air (reps should total 25-100).

Day 4: Warm Up, Cardio, and Relaxation

How can one exercise be all three: warm up, cardo, and a relaxer? As simple as this program is, it must be experienced to realize it. This is another specialty of the exercise master... the toddler. Jump, jump. I am only speaking of a millimeter or less. It should be barely perceivable that you are leaving the ground. It is even possible to not jump, but come very close to jumping, in order to progress to leaving the ground. If this jump is too challenging, jump from one foot to another as if running in place (or place each foot down with no jump and run in place) at your own pace.

This exercise is like jumping rope without any rope. It is certainly okay to use rope if it does not frustrate you or impede constant movement. Jump like this for as many seconds as possible and document how long you lasted. Rest for half as many seconds and jump again for as long as you did on your first set. Repeat this process for ten minutes or as close to it as possible.

Be sure to relax the arms and every muscle you can think of in the body while jumping. Start by focusing on relaxing the muscles that are definitely not needed for jumping, such as the fingers.

If you cannot do this for ten minutes, or if you wish to experience a deeper sense of relaxation, shake out your arms and legs. Set your 10 minute timer and attempt to jump the entire time with intervals of shaking out the arms and legs if you need a rest.

That's it for today, one exercise... jumping. There are books on jumping rope for health and theories on how the cell is completely relaxed in between the up and down phase of jumping. I have even been told that over 72 positive genes are activated during this process. Jumping for only 2 minutes increases bone density. Calcium cannot be absorbed into the bone without weight bearing exercises.

Consider this study, as this is one of many on bone density increasing with jumping a very small amount. "Sixty premenopausal women, ages 25 to 50, significantly increased their hip bone mineral density after four months by .5% by jumping 10 times a day, twice a day and taking short breaks (30 seconds) between each jump." Doesn't sound like a lot of gain? Consider this: the controls lost about 1.3% of their bone density over the same period. "Women jumped as high as they could from the floor," says lead study researcher Larry Tucker, PhD. No box, shoes, or pads were used." -By Linda Melone, CSCS Mar 12, 2014 www.Prevention.com

Day 5: Let's Make Week One Strong

7 exercises:

- ☐ Micro-Jump in Place
- ☐ Squats
- ☐ Dand
- ☐ Back Extension
- ☐ N Up
- ☐ Modified Cobra
- ☐ Split Sitting

Do each exercise for 30-60 seconds. If you can not do each exercise more than 15 seconds, either make your range of motion smaller or simply complete an extra set of each. This workout should take 7 minutes and no longer than 10 minutes, if it takes longer then analyze your break times to be sure you are not resting more than 5 seconds in between each exercise.

Day 6: Rest, meditate, and breathe deeply

If you are feeling pumped up and want to exercise, simply breathe deep and practice the breathing exercises again. You can also research more about health, preferably through a textbook or as legitimate of a source as you can.

Drink as many ounces of water that equals half of what you weigh in pounds (or more if thirsty), sometimes an attractive container to drink out of makes all the difference.

Day 7: The Trinity of Exercises

- ☐ Squat
- ☐ Dand
- ☐ Back Extension

Perform one exercise after another with as little rest as possible, being sure not to rest longer than 30 seconds for maximum results. Use your timer to be sure that you are performing at least 30% of your max, for example if you did the dand and squatted for 1 minute each as your max, then execute the squat for 20 seconds and then go directly to the dand for 20 seconds. Be sure to move cautiously from one exercise to another without taking an extended rest.

Perform these three exercises: the squat, the dand, and the back extension non stop for ten minutes going from one exercise to another and then repeating the process.

Enjoy your ten minutes as you enjoy your breakfast, and the way a toddler enjoys each and every strenuous movement knowing that we are growing and regenerating constantly. Realize you are getting better and better every day. Breathe deep during your workouts, and be sure to get proper rejuvenation daily with as much sleep as possible during the night. During true rest is when your muscles heal and regenerate from the micro-tears, and this is when your muscles grow or become more dense and functional.

Day 8: Maximum Respect

How much do you respect yourself? Answer that question by being willing to do as many repetitions of one exercise as you are capable. Do as many squats as you can in 10 minutes taking as little breaks as possible. Realize if you practice these exercises for one year consistently for only ten minutes, no matter what level you are currently at, you will be able to squat for ten minutes non stop!

It is only ten minutes. You have 1,440 minutes every day. This is only ten of them.

Your heart rate should increase as if you are running, and perspiration should match that.

Do not overly concern yourself if your range of motion is not so big, even if you have trouble sitting on the chair. Progressively work up to squatting on the chair and then past it, yet do not hesitate to perform the squat with a one inch movement. Keep the form perfect by keeping your back straight and observing toddlers squat. You can also observe adults who squat almost as well as toddlers.

Day 9: It's All In Your Mind

Another day to show your respect for yourself. Show yourself how much you love yourself and how hard you are willing to work for what you love.

Maximum repetitions of dand in ten minutes. This workout may not seem like the most exciting, and the mind can wander to think about all the fancy machines and different exercises one can do. This is the same negative thoughts that may come up while doing any exercise, which is different from activity because it is planned. This sometimes can make a workout more challenging. I once heard from a man who runs over 50 miles at a time, and sets records, that the hardest part of a run is to tie his sneakers.

Just do it and reap the glorious results. Do it for who you love and all the toys you like to play with. Do as many repetitions as you can within ten minutes with as little rest as possible between sets.

Day 10: Core Strength and Stretch for Strength

- ☐   N Up
- ☐   Back Extension
- ☐   Modified Cobra
- ☐   Split

Practice the N Up and the Back Extension for 30-60 seconds each and then practice these two stretches one after another. Use the prescription mentioned for the split on Day 3, 10 second hold, 5 seconds of conscious tension, 10 seconds stretch again yet a bit further, 5 seconds tension, and 10 seconds stretch even a bit further. The modified cobra prescription is a 4 minute hold.

Day 11: 10 10 wins

- ☐ Jump in place
- ☐ Squat
- ☐ Dand
- ☐ N Up
- ☐ Back Extension

Simple and effective. Focus your mind on how you will look, feel, and think after thirty days of training, or even after these ten minutes. You are only doing ten repetitions. Ten reps of each exercise one after another for ten minutes. Little to no rest in between exercises, in fact make the transition from one exercise to another exercise an exercise itself, perfecting the smoothness of the transition every time.

Day 12: 100 percent sure

To celebrate 12 days let's get to 100 repetitions of the two foundational exercises in the program. 100 squats and 100 dands in ten minutes. Ten minutes is plenty of time to compete 200 reps. This may be a faster pace than you have been currently performing, yet you have conditioned your body and it is time to condition your mind and take your health to the next level.

Alternate from one exercise to another yet be sure to complete at least ten repetitions of each exercise before you move on to the next. Rip a piece of paper into 20 pieces (or use 20 pieces of something with each piece representing 10 reps) and move them from one bowl or place to another. Each piece will represent 10 reps. This is an easy way to keep count during exertion when it is best you focus on your goal and not on counting.

For an increased challenge and conditioning, perform 100 reps non stop of the squat then the dand. Your form must be perfect for every rep, even the last one. Even if you modify the exercises to be a smaller range of motion, they can still be perfect as long as you are focusing on your goal, have stacked joints (a straight back and knee just about over the ankle), feel the burn, and breathe heavy.

Pant and burn. You should be breathing very heavy during every workout, especially this one on day 12 due to you having proper conditioning now. You should be panting, yet able to speak properly and hold a conversation. You should also feel a burning sensation localized to the muscle(s) you are working. These two things are very important as emphasized in this program. Pant and burn.

Day 13: Smile, You Are on Camera

I did not want to overwhelm you with too much information at once, so I left this detail for day 13. Be sure to smile during every workout. This is absolutely essential. You smile for a camera most likely, why not smile for the most important person that you see 24/7? You are doing this for yourself, to be healthier, happier, and stronger, so what better way to express yourself than to smile? Smile as if you completed your goal, because making it this far is truly revolutionary.

- ☐ Smile
- ☐ Jump
- ☐ Squat with (micro) jump
- ☐ N Up
- ☐ Split (stretch)
- ☐ Back Extension
- ☐ Modified Cobra (stretch)

Do 5 exercises for 15 seconds each: Jump, Squat with a tiny jump at the top, N Up, Split, and Back Extension and repeat once. Then cool down with the Modified Cobra for 4 minutes.

Day 14: Rejoice and Rest

Today practice deep breathing more than your current discipline of once per day minimum. Rest and go into nature to contemplate how much you have accomplished. Go barefoot, or sit on the bare Earth (cloth is ok) to experience "grounding" your electrical current.

Day 15: Simplify

- ☐ Jump
- ☐ Squat
- ☐ Dand
- ☐ Back Extension
- ☐ N Up
- ☐ Split
- ☐ Modified Cobra

Smile during the whole workout as if it is the best day of your life.

Perform each exercise for 30 seconds, except for the stretches: the split and the modified cobra.

Repeat if you "feel good," and do three sets if you "feel great".

This should take 5-10 minutes, or more if you feel so good you do not wish to stop.

Cool down with the two stretches as prescribed:
-Split for 10 seconds, 5 second tension, 10 seconds deeper stretch, and repeat twice.
-Modified Cobra for 4 minutes.

This is how simple your workout is and can be to be in the best shape of your life.

Day 16: Keep it Simple

- ☐ Jump
- ☐ Squat
- ☐ Dand
- ☐ Back Extension
- ☐ N Up

Do every exercise for 10 seconds.

Repeat 5-10 times, or however many times you can do this in ten minutes.

Day 17: Simpler

Realize how simple it is to fully exert your muscles if you put your mind to it and you have the proper exercises and consistency.

- ☐ Jump
- ☐ Squat
- ☐ Dand

Do each exercise for 30 seconds until your 10 minute timer goes off.

Day 18: Simple and much easier

- ☐ N Up
- ☐ Back Extension
- ☐ Split
- ☐ Modified Cobra

Practice the N up and back extension for 30-60 seconds each then follow the stretching protocol.

-Split for 10 seconds, 5 second tension, 10 seconds deeper stretch, and repeat twice.
-Modified Cobra for 4 minutes.

Repeat until your ten minute timer goes off.

Day 19: Freedom of Movement

Only 20 repetitions for this workout. 20 jumps, 20 squats, 20 dands, 20 back extensions, and 20 N Ups and then repeat. Do this for ten minutes. Play your favorite music and feel as if you are dancing.

Remember you can always adjust the range of motion so that the exercise is not only possible, but it is easy, especially compared to a full deep range of motion. The important thing is that you do it.

Day 20: Do you remember?

Do you remember the exercises in the program? How many are there?

- ☐ Jump
- ☐ Squat
- ☐ Dand
- ☐ Back Extension
- ☐ N Up
- ☐ Split
- ☐ Modified Cobra

Do each exercise for as long as you feel comfortable and then do what you remember of the stretching protocol. Document how long this workout took in your journal and be sure to write how you felt before and after the workout emotionally and mentally on a scale of 1-100.

Day 21: Love the Life You Live

Create a workout from the 5 exercises and 2 stretches, it is okay if you do not do more than one exercise also.

Put the timer on for 10 minutes and listen to great music, realizing that, if you choose it to be, this can be the best day of your life, until tomorrow.

Day 22: Drink Up

Today is the day to write a bit more in your journal. Write down what increases your Natural Health and what is robbing you of health. 2 lists, read them, and check them twice. That is all for the journal.

Now for the workout:

-Jump for 2 minutes.
-Squat for 3 minutes.
-Dand for 1 minute.
-Back Extension for 1 minute.
-N Up for 1 minute.
-Modified Cobra for 2 minutes.

Day 23: Inherit your inner child

Remember your toddler days. Squat for 10 minutes with plenty of holds at the bottom of the squat, like a child on our royal throne. In fact, you can hold the squat in your Royal Throne, at the bottom of the squat, for 10 minutes as an excellent workout.

If you need a break, practice active recovery and perform N ups or back extensions as an active rest for your legs.

Day 24: Open your Heart

Remember to pull back your shoulders and pull your shoulder blades towards each other, "opening your heart", during the exercises and during the day for optimal posture.

Dand for 10 minutes with plenty of holds at the top and bottom of the dand, like a child when they go into pyramid, and pretend it is a rest.

If you need a break, practice active recovery and perform N ups or back extensions as an active rest for your chest.

Day 25: Rest Before the Test

The point of this rest is to address two issues:
- It is okay to rest a day if you are consistent for 90% of your time.
- It is important to rest to fully heal, most athletes know to rest before a game for optimal performance.

Practice as much deep and active breathing as possible today.

Day 26: You are now fit

If you made it this far, you are doing amazing and have definitely increased your fitness level tremendously in just ten minutes per day. If your range of motion is not full, you may be hesitating to push yourself to your sub maximal efforts (anaerobic threshold) which is imperative to growth. It is never too late to push yourself to your limits safely. In fact, it is NOT very safe at all to NOT push your limits, as many studies show, time and time again.

Today is another day for 3 digits. The 100 club. The 100 squats are to be done in one set, adjusting range of motion if needed. The 100 dands are to be done in no more than 10 sets with the same number of back extensions as an active recovery. If you are having trouble with form, remember to adjust the range of motion. You can also take 10 seconds to breathe as deeply as possible. 10 seconds rest will help to regenerate the high energy phosphate bond (A.T.P) that is responsible for the burst of energy needed for the exercise. Every second matters.

Day 27: Cadence

Cadence is like dancing, it is simply to keep a beat, or rythically continuing at the same pace. Today you will keep a cadence with all your exercises.

- ☐ Jump
- ☐ Squat
- ☐ Dand
- ☐ N Up
- ☐ Back Extension

Do each exercise for 30 seconds at a comfortable pace, then double the pace for 15 seconds.

Cool down with modified cobra for 4 minutes.

Day 28: Study

Today is a research day. Learn more about Natural Health. Research Wimm Hoff, or read a textbook about health. Watch some calisthenics videos, or read a book about health you have been neglecting. This is an essential step in anyone's health journey to continue to feed the will with knowledge.

Do not take this as an inactive day. Either dance or play with activity intense enough to noticeably raise your heart rate, or do 100 squats throughout the day.

Day 29: 200

Do 200 Squats throughout the day. This method is called GTW, Greasing The Wheel. It is another Russian secret training method that turns muscles into elastic steel; which they are! It basically means to practice a particular exercise often and through the day. For example, every time you enter or exit your residence, do 10 to 50 squats. Do this for a month and you will see enormous gains.

Day 30: Congratulations

You have accomplished a great feat, please keep up the excellence. I hope that I showed you enough combinations of these amazing exercises to free you from the confines of a sedentary life, or thinking we need equipment or gyms to be in superb health. Continue to learn. Continue to practice and learn new exercises to broaden your training, and keep your mind entertained with new and exciting workouts. These exercises were chosen for their effectiveness and combined to efficiently increase health in the entire body.

Today's workout is to see how many of each exercise you are capable of after 30 days of training on the Natural Health Program. Please document your results and send them to OGFit.com.

Document this in your Natural Health Journey Journal and bask in the glory of the progress you have made in 30 days.

Thank You. Blessed Love and Gratitude,
Keith Lopez of www.OGFit.com

www.ingramcontent.com/pod-product-compliance
Lightning Source LLC
Chambersburg PA
CBHW060327240426
43665CB00047B/2811